Aus der Reihe:
English - quite easy

Friedhelm Heitmann

All about jobs

Band 5

Übungsmaterial zum Einsatz im elementaren Förderunterricht zum Erlernen der englischen Sprache

Lernen mit Erfolg
KOHL VERLAG
Der Verlag mit dem Baum
www.kohlverlag.de

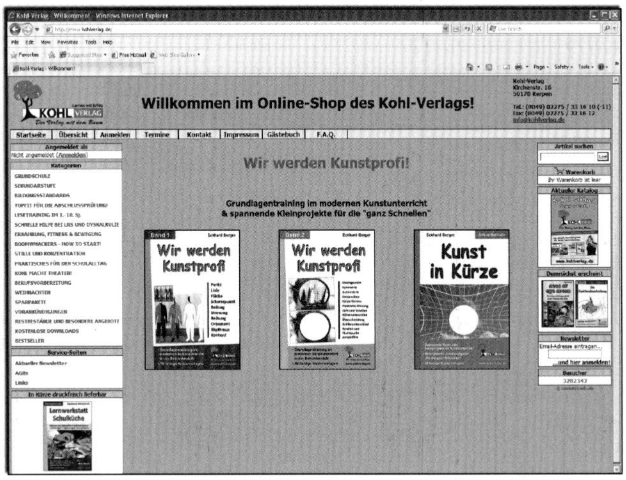

English - quite easy (Band 5)
- All about jobs -

1. Auflage 2009

Inhalt: Friedhelm Heitmann
Grafik & Satz: Kohl-Verlag
Druck: Orths Medien GmbH

Bestell-Nr. 10 939

ISBN: 3-86632-939-3
ISBN-13: 978-3-86632-939-3

Inhalt

		page
Vorwort		4
Didaktische und methodische Hinweise		5
1.	Dream Jobs – a game	6
2.	"Ordinary" jobs	7
3.	Can you find out the job?	8 - 9
4.	Working people	10
5.	Jobs from A to Z	11
6.	At work	12
7.	Tools	13
8.	Who works with ...	14 - 15
9.	Computers	16
10.	Questions	17
11.	A typical workday	18
12.	The world of jobs (adjectives)	19
13.	Present simple - Present progressive - Past simple	20 - 21
14.	Opposites	22 - 23
15.	Expectations	24
16.	Informations about a job	25
17.	Practical training (work experience)	26 - 27
18.	An interview in a company	28 - 29
19.	At work (work experience, training, job ...)	30
20.	Getting a job	31 - 32
21.	Finding a job	33
22.	Application	34
23.	Curriculum vitae	35
24.	An interview	36 - 37
25.	All about my favourite job	38
26.	The world of jobs	39
27.	My life in ten years	40
28.	Vocabulary test	41
29.	"What do you know about ...?" – a game	42 - 43
30.	Repetition	44 - 52
31.	Class test 1	53 - 57
32.	Class test 2	58 - 62
33.	The answers	63 - 67

KOHL VERLAG Der Verlag mit dem Baum www.kohlverlag.de
English: quite easy / Band 5
All about jobs - Bestell-Nr. 10 939

Vorwort

Liebe Kolleginnen und Kollegen,

Englisch ist eine Weltsprache, man kann sie auch als „Weltsprache Nr. 1“ bezeichnen. Weltweit wird in der englischen Sprache im privaten und öffentlichen Leben kommuniziert. Englisch ist in vielfältigen Lebenssituationen anzutreffen. Diese Sprache gilt als leicht zu erlernende Sprache, zumindest wird dies wiederholt behauptet. Der Schulalltag zeigt jedoch: Manche Schülerinnen und Schüler haben große Schwierigkeiten mit dem Englischen.

Vor diesem Hintergrund entstand die von mir verfasste Reihe „English - quite easy“, in der in kleinen Schritten „step by step“ vorgegangen wird. Die vorliegenden Bände sind vorgesehen für Anfänger, sie sind konzipiert für den elementaren Förderunterricht. Die dargebotenen Arbeitsblätter gingen aus der Schulpraxis hervor – und zwar aus der langjährigen Arbeit mit Haupt- und Förderschülern. Diese verfügten zunächst – bei Beginn des Unterrichts – über keine oder nur geringe Englischkenntnisse.

Die vorliegenden Kopiervorlagen sind jederzeit veränder- und erweiterbar. Weitere Anregungen sind dabei gern willkommen.

Viel Freude und Erfolg beim Einsatz der vorliegenden Kopiervorlagen wünschen Ihnen der Kohl-Verlag und

Friedhelm Heitmann

<u>Die Reihe „English – quite easy“ besteht bisher aus folgenden sechs Bänden</u>:

• **<u>Band 1</u>: Let's start to speak English**	**Nr. 10 805**	**12,90 €**
• **<u>Band 2</u>: Let's go on speaking English**	**Nr. 10 806**	**12,90 €**
• **<u>Band 3</u>: Grammar for beginners**	**Nr. 10 848**	**12,90 €**
• **<u>Band 4</u>: From Germany to the United Kingdom**	**Nr. 10 849**	**12,90 €**
• **<u>Band 5</u>: All about jobs**	**Nr. 10 939**	**14,90 €**
• **<u>Band 6</u>: All about teenagers**	**Nr. 10 940**	**13,90 €**

Didaktische und methodische Hinweise

Die präsentierten Bände dienen der Vermittlung, Festigung und Überprüfung elementarer Grundkenntnisse der englischen Sprache. Je nach Bedarf oder Wunsch lassen sich die Bände ganz oder in Auszügen (Schwerpunkte daraus bzw. einzelne Seiten) verwenden. Die Werke eignen sich in kompletter Form für Schülerinnen und Schüler im herkömmlichen Unterricht sowie im Rahmen der Wochenplanarbeit und Freiarbeit. Sowohl für einzelne Schülerinnen und Schüler als auch für die gesamte Klasse können die direkt einsetzbaren Vorlagen benutzt werden.

Einerseits sind die Arbeitsblätter gewöhnlich schnell überschaubar, zum anderen bieten sie genügend Platz für schriftliche Eintragungen. Die Schülerinnen und Schüler benötigen dafür keine weiteren Einzelblätter, Schreibblöcke oder Hefte. Auf vielen Arbeitsblättern werden als Hilfestellung beispielsweise Satzanfänge oder ungeordnete Lösungshinweise vorgegeben.

Im Anschluss an die Arbeitsblätter gibt es in jedem Band zwei Leistungskontrollen, die im Unterricht als Tests oder Klassenarbeiten eingesetzt werden können. Dabei können jeweils 100 Punkte erzielt werden.

Im Anhang zum Band sind die Lösungen zu den einzelnen Arbeitsblättern und Leistungskontrollen aufgelistet. Ideal ist es, wenn der Lehrer/die Lehrerin den Schülerinnen und Schülern die Gelegenheit gibt, ihre Antworten selbst im Anhang zu überprüfen.

Genug der Vorbemerkungen! Die folgenden Materialien sprechen für sich, sodass ganz bewusst auf weitere didaktische und methodische Anmerkungen verzichtet wird. Letztlich bleibt es den Lehrerinnen und Lehrern überlassen, welche der hier vorgestellten Materialien sie in den Unterricht aufnehmen.

1 Dream Jobs – a game

Exercise 1: *Dreams are not forbidden. You can choose 3 from the following 20 dream jobs. What do you want to be?*

- actor/actress
- artist
- basketball star
- comic actor/comic actress
- detective
- football star
- motorcyclist
- pilot
- singer
- tennis star
- architect
- astronaut
- boxer
- computer expert
- doctor
- model
- racing driver
- scientist
- news presenter
- writer

My 1. dream job: ______________________________

My 2. dream job: ______________________________

My 3. dream job: ______________________________

The pupils have to guess which job the others have choosed. The person who calls out the right answer first wins a point. Who wins the most points?

Other dream jobs:

____

____

____

____

____

English: quite easy / Band 5
All about jobs - Bestell-Nr. 10 939
KOHL VERLAG Der Verlag mit dem Baum
www.kohlverlag.de

2 "Ordinary" jobs

Exercise 1: *Translate into the German language.*

a) baker ⇨ ______________

b) bank clerk ⇨ ______________

c) bricklayer ⇨ ______________

d) butcher ⇨ ______________

e) car mechanic ⇨ ______________

f) carpenter ⇨ ______________

g) cashier ⇨ ______________

h) cleaner ⇨ ______________

i) cook ⇨ ______________

j) dentist ⇨ ______________

k) doctor ⇨ ______________

l) doctor's assistant ⇨ ______________

m) dressmaker ⇨ ______________

n) gardener ⇨ ______________

o) hairdresser ⇨ ______________

p) housewife ⇨ ______________

q) joiner ⇨ ______________

r) nurse ⇨ ______________

s) painter ⇨ ______________

t) policeman ⇨ ______________

u) postman ⇨ ______________

v) shop assistant ⇨ ______________

w) taxi driver ⇨ ______________

x) teacher ⇨ ______________

y) waiter/waitress ⇨ ______________

Exercise 2: **a)** *You need a job to earn money. What kind of work would you like to do?*

____

b) *What is your father's job?*

____

c) *What is your mother's job?*

____

d) *What are your sisters and brothers working?*

____

____

KOHL VERLAG Der Verlag mit dem Baum www.kohlverlag.de
English: quite easy / Band 5 - Bestell-Nr. 10 939
All about jobs

3 Can you find out the job?

<u>Exercise 1</u>: *Write down the names of the jobs.*

Answers:

architect - baker - bank clerk - bricklayer - car mechanic - carpenter - cashier - cleaner - cook - dentist - doctor - doctor's assistant - dressmaker - gardener - hairdresser - housewife - joiner - nurse - painter - policeman - postman - shop assistant - taxi driver - teacher - waitress/waiter

	A person who ... :	... is a(n):
a)	medicates ill people	
b)	helps you when you have toothache	
c)	assists the doctor	
d)	cares for ill people (female person)	
e)	gives lessons at school	
f)	controlls the public order	
g)	works in a bank	
h)	collects money	
i)	sells things or goods in a shop	
j)	plans buildings	
k)	builds the walls of houses	
l)	builds the roof of a house	
m)	makes tables, chairs, doors out of timber	
n)	works with brushes and colours	
o)	keeps clean rooms	
p)	makes bread	

KOHL VERLAG Der Verlag mit dem Baum
English: quite easy / Band 5
All about jobs - Bestell-Nr. 10 939
www.kohlverlag.de

3 Can you find out the job?

	A person who ... :	... is a(n):
q)	prepares food	
r)	serves food and drinks in a restaurant	
s)	cuts hair	
t)	makes clothes	
u)	delivers letters and parcels	
v)	drives people by car	
w)	repairs cars	
x)	looks after the plants in parks	
y)	cares for the family	

Exercise 2: *Write own sentences.*

Example: A butcher cuts meat.

English: quite easy / Band 5
All about jobs - Bestell-Nr. 10 939
KOHL VERLAG
www.kohlverlag.de

4 Working people

<u>Exercise 1</u>: *Try to find out what the people in the pictures are working. What's the name of the job?*

baker - butcher - data typist - drawer - farmer - florist - joiner - manager - machine fitter - photographer - physiotherapist - secretary - typesetter - waiter

1. 	2. 	3. 	4. 	5. 
6. 	7. 	8. 	9. 	10. 
11. 	12. 	13. 	14. 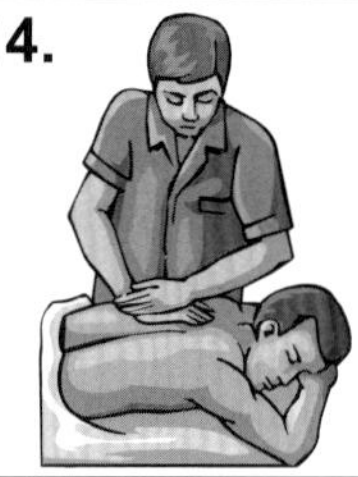	

1. ____________________ 8. ____________________

2. ____________________ 9. ____________________

3. ____________________ 10. ____________________

4. ____________________ 11. ____________________

5. ____________________ 12. ____________________

6. ____________________ 13. ____________________

7. ____________________ 14. ____________________

KOHL VERLAG Der Verlag mit dem Baum www.kohlverlag.de
English: quite easy / Band 5
All about jobs - Bestell-Nr. 10 939

5 Jobs from A to Z

<u>Exercise 1</u>: *What jobs do you know? Play the game according the game „City, State, River, ...“.*

First letter:

a or b:

c or d:

e or f:

g or h:

i or j:

k or l:

m or n:

o or p:

r or s:

t or u:

v or w or z:

English: quite easy / Band 5
All about jobs - Bestell-Nr. 10 939
KOHL VERLAG Der Verlag mit dem Baum
www.kohlverlag.de

6 At work

Exercise 1: *What do working people do?*
Write down complete sentences.

a) They ... ____________________

b) They ... ____________________

c) They ... ____________________

d) They ... ____________________

e) They ... ____________________

f) They ... ____________________

g) They ... ____________________

h) They ... ____________________

i) They ... ____________________

j) They ... ____________________

k) They ... ____________________

l) They ... ____________________

m) They ... ____________________

n) They ... ____________________

o) They ... ____________________

p) They ... ____________________

q) They ... ____________________

r) They ... ____________________

s) They ... ____________________

t) They ... ____________________

u) They ... ____________________

v) They ... ____________________

w) They ... ____________________

x) They ... ____________________

KOHL VERLAG Der Verlag mit dem Baum
English: quite easy / Band 5
All about jobs - Bestell-Nr. 10 939
www.kohlverlag.de

7 Tools

Exercise 1: *What does it mean in German?*

a) axe ⇨ ________________
b) broom ⇨ ________________
c) comb ⇨ ________________
d) crowbar ⇨ ________________
e) drill ⇨ ________________
f) file ⇨ ________________
g) folding rule ⇨ ________________
h) fork ⇨ ________________
i) hammer ⇨ ________________
j) knife ⇨ ________________
k) needle ⇨ ________________
l) paint brush ⇨ ________________
m) pincers ⇨ ________________
n) pitchfork ⇨ ________________
o) rake ⇨ ________________
p) saw ⇨ ________________
q) scissors ⇨ ________________
r) screwdriver ⇨ ________________
s) shovel ⇨ ________________
t) spade ⇨ ________________
u) spanner ⇨ ________________
v) scraper ⇨ ________________
w) spirit level ⇨ ________________
x) spoon ⇨ ________________
y) trowel ⇨ ________________

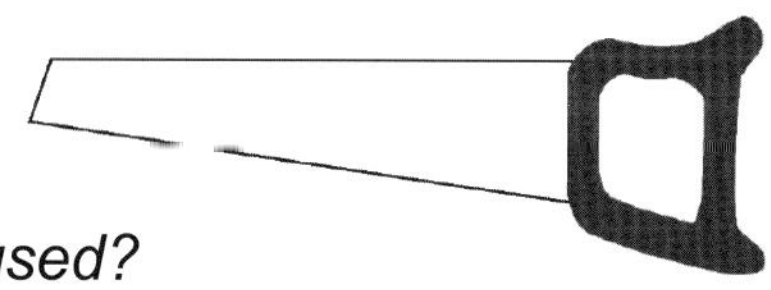

Exercise 2: **a)** *Which of these tools have you already used?*

____

____

____

b) *Which tools may be in a tool bag?*

____

____

____

c) *Which other tools do you know?*

____

____

English: quite easy / Band 5
All about jobs - Bestell-Nr. 10 939
KOHL VERLAG Der Verlag mit dem Baum
www.kohlverlag.de

8 Who works with ...

Exercise 1: *Answer in complete sentences.*

Example: A teacher works with a pen.

a) *Who works with an axe?*

____

b) *Who works with a comb?*

____

c) *Who works with a drill?*

____

d) *Who works with a file?*

____

e) *Who works with a fork?*

____

f) *Who works with a hammer?*

____

g) *Who works with a knife?*

____

h) *Who works with a needle?*

____

i) *Who works with a paint brush?*

____

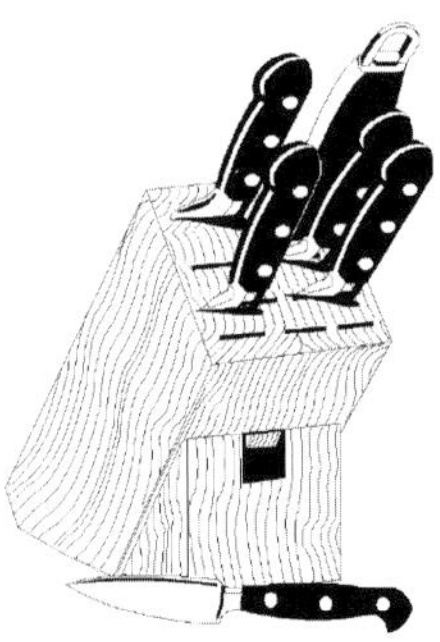

j) *Who works with a rake?*

____

k) *Who works with a saw?*

____

KOHL VERLAG
www.kohlverlag.de
English: quite easy / Band 5
All about jobs - Bestell-Nr. 10 939

8 Who works with ...

l) *Who works with a scissors?*

____

m) *Who works with a screwdriver?*

____

n) *Who works with a spoon?*

____

o) *Who works with a trowel?*

____

Exercise 2: *Write own sentences.*

Example: A house wife works with a broom.

English: quite easy / Band 5
All about jobs - Bestell-Nr. 10 939
KOHL VERLAG
www.kohlverlag.de

9 Computers

In the working world you find computers almost everywhere. You should be able to use a computer.

Exercise 1: *Look at the picture. There are 14 items. What is what?*

desktop - disks - joystick - keyboard - modem - mouse - mouse pad - printer - processor - scanner - screen - swivel chair - speaker - web camera

1. ______________________ 8. ______________________

2. ______________________ 9. ______________________

3. ______________________ 10. ______________________

4. ______________________ 11. ______________________

5. ______________________ 12. ______________________

6. ______________________ 13. ______________________

7. ______________________ 14. ______________________

English: quite easy / Band 5
All about jobs - Bestell-Nr. 10 939
KOHL VERLAG Der Verlag mit dem Baum
www.kohlverlag.de

10 Questions

Exercise 1: *Answer the following questions in complete sentences.*

a) *What can you do with a computer?*

____

____

____

b) *For what do you need a computer?*

____

____

____

c) *What do you think is a "computer freak"?*

____

____

____

Rund um den Computer

abbrechen	abort, cancel	Maus	mouse
abspeichern	save	Mauspad	mouse pad
abstürzen	crash	Menüleiste	menu bar
anklicken	click (on)	Modem	modem
Bildschirm	monitor, screen	Ordner	folder
Bildschirmschoner	screen saver	Pfad	path
CD-ROM-Laufwerk	CD-ROM drive	Schnittstelle	interface
Datei	file	Soundkarte	sound card
Drucker	printer	speichern	save (to)
entfernen	delete	Symbolleiste	toolbar
Fenster	window	Tastatur	keyboard
Festplatte	hard disk	Treiber	driver
formatieren	format	Zwischenablage	clipboard
Laufwerk	drive		

KOHL VERLAG www.kohlverlag.de
English: quite easy / Band 5
All about jobs - Bestell-Nr. 10 939

11 A typical workday

Exercise 1: *Adam is out of work.*
Imagine how he spends his time!

a) *Adam gets up at ...*

____

b) *Then ...*

____

c) *After that ...*

____

d) *Later on ...*

____

e) *At last ...*

____

Exercise 2: *Betty is a trainee. She works in a shop. Imagine how she spends her workday!*

a) *Betty wakes up ...*

____

b) *Afterwards ...*

____

c) *Next ...*

____

d) *In the evening ...*

____

e) *Finally ...*

____

English: quite easy / Band 5
All about jobs - Bestell-Nr. 10 939
KOHL VERLAG Der Verlag mit dem Baum
www.kohlverlag.de

12 The world of jobs (adjectives)

Exercise 1: *Translate into German.*

Characteristics you should have ...

a) punctual	⇨	____________
b) friendly	⇨	____________
c) polite	⇨	____________
d) honest	⇨	____________
e) reliable	⇨	____________
f) careful	⇨	____________
g) clean	⇨	____________
h) helpful	⇨	____________
i) attentive	⇨	____________
j) busy	⇨	____________
k) responsible	⇨	____________
l) flexible	⇨	____________
m) cooperative	⇨	____________
n) powerful	⇨	____________
o) resistant	⇨	____________
p) tireless	⇨	____________
q) well-organized	⇨	____________
r) clever	⇨	____________
s) self-confident	⇨	____________
t) independent	⇨	____________

Exercise 2: *Which of these characteristics do you have?*
Write down complete sentences!

KOHL VERLAG Der Verlag mit dem Baum
www.kohlverlag.de
English: quite easy / Band 5
All about jobs - Bestell-Nr. 10 939

13 Present simple - Present progressive - Past simple

Exercise 1: *Turn the following sentences from present simple into Present progressive.*

a) PS: I earn a little money in a shop.

PP: ______________________________

b) PS: The men work in a hall.

PP: ______________________________

c) PS: The women clean the classrooms.

PP: ______________________________

d) PS: The trainer talks to a trainee.

PP: ______________________________

e) PS: Some boys and girls job during the holiday.

PP: ______________________________

f) PS: George applies for a job.

PP: ______________________________

g) PS: Ann writes an application.

PP: ______________________________

h) PS: Ron goes to the job centre.

PP: ______________________________

i) PS: The pupils gain first working experience.

PP: ______________________________

j) PS: They get informations about the world of jobs.

PP: ______________________________

English: quite easy / Band 5
All about jobs - Bestell-Nr. 10 939
KOHL VERLAG Der Verlag mit dem Baum
www.kohlverlag.de

13 Present simple - Present progressive - Past simple

Exercise 2: *Now turn the sentences into Past simple.*

a) ______________________________

b) ______________________________

c) ______________________________

d) ______________________________

e) ______________________________

f) ______________________________

g) ______________________________

h) ______________________________

i) ______________________________

j) ______________________________

Exercise 3:
- *Write own sentences about the world of jobs.*
- *First note down the sentences in Present simple.*
- *After that note down in Present progressive.*
- *Finally note down in Past simple.*

____

____

____

____

____

____

____

____

____

____

KOHL VERLAG Der Verlag mit dem Baum www.kohlverlag.de
English: quite easy / Band 5
All about jobs - Bestell-Nr. 10 939

14 Opposites

Exercise 1: *Do you know the opposites? Fill in.*

demand (Nachfrage) - cashless (bargeldlos) - dishonest (unehrlich) - dismiss (entlassen) - employee (Arbeitnehmerin, Arbeitnehmer) - leisure time (Freizeit) - lazy (faul) - loss (Verlust) - male worker (Arbeiter) - night shift (Nachtschicht) - ordinary job (gewöhnlicher Beruf) - part-time job (Teilzeitbeschäftigung) - sale (Verkauf) - to be out of work (arbeitslos sein) - trainee (Auszubildender, Auszubildende) - unfit for work (arbeitsunfähig) - unpunctual (unpünktlich) - work-shy (arbeitsscheu)

a) *The opposite of* **work** *(Arbeit) is* ______________________ .

b) *The opposite of* **having a job** *(Arbeit haben) is* ____________________ .

c) *The opposite of* **day shift** *(Tagschicht) is* _____________________ .

d) *The opposite of a* **dream job** *(Traumberuf) is* ______________________ .

e) *The opposite of an* **employer** *(Arbeitgeberin, Arbeitgeber) is* ______________ .

f) *The opposite of a* **female worker** *(Arbeiterin) is* ___________________ .

g) *The opposite of a* **full-time job** *(Vollzeitbeschäftigung) is a* _________________ .

h) *The opposite of* **fit for work** *(arbeitsfähig) is* ___________________ .

i) *The opposite of* **punctual** *(pünktlich) is* ___________________ .

j) *The opposite of* **busy** *(fleißig) is* ___________________ .

k) *The opposite of* **honest** *(ehrlich) is* ___________________ .

l) *The opposite of* **willing to work** *(arbeitswillig) is* ___________________ .

m) *The opposite of* **to hire** *(anstellen) is to* ___________________ .

n) *The opposite of a* **trainer** *(Ausbilder) is a* ____________________ .

o) *The opposite of* **profit** *(Gewinn) is* ______________________ .

p) *The opposite of* **offer** *(Angebot) is* ______________________ .

q) *The opposite of* **buying** *(Einkauf) is* _______________________ .

r) *The opposite of* **in cash** *(bar) is* _______________________ .

English: quite easy / Band 5
All about jobs - Bestell-Nr. 10 939
KOHL VERLAG Der Verlag mit dem Baum
www.kohlverlag.de

14 Opposites

Exercise 2: *Answer the following questions in complete sentences.*

a) *Are you fit for work?*

b) *Are you unpunctual?*

c) *Are you lazy?*

d) *Are you honest?*

e) *Do you like working at night?*

f) *Do you prefer working inside or outside?*

g) *Would you like to become an employer or an employee?*

Exercise 3: **a)** *What are you good at? What are you bad at?*

I am good at ...	I am bad at ...

b) *What jobs do you like?*

KOHL VERLAG
Der Verlag mit dem Baum
www.kohlverlag.de
English: quite easy / Band 5
All about jobs - Bestell-Nr. 10 939

15 Expectations

What do you expect from your job?

- “The job must be interesting.“
- “I want to have a regular employment.“
- “I hope I don‘t have to work too hard.“
- “I need a rest.“
- “I want to earn a lot of money.“
- “There are chances to be promoted.“
- “It is a respected job.“
- “I have a lot of fun at work.“
- “I like to work together with nice people.“
- “I have got various duties.“

<u>Exercise 1</u>: *What is (most) important for you? Give your ranking!*

1. position: ______________________________

2. position: ______________________________

3. position: ______________________________

4. position: ______________________________

5. position: ______________________________

6. position: ______________________________

7. position: ______________________________

8. position: ______________________________

9. position: ______________________________

10. position: ______________________________

Other expectations:

____

____

____

____

KOHL VERLAG Der Verlag mit dem Baum
www.kohlverlag.de
English: quite easy / Band 5
All about jobs - Bestell-Nr. 10 939

16 Informations about a job

Exercise 1: *Imagine you are looking for a job. Answer in whole sentences.*

a) What kind of job are you interested in?

I am interested in ______________________________

____

b) How many hours do you have to work daily and weekly in this job?

I have to work ______________________________

____

c) How much money could you earn in this job?

I could earn about ______________________________

d) How long will the job training be?

The job training will take ______________________________

____

e) What are your duties in this job?

You make ______________________________

____

f) What tools and machines do you have to use in this job?

I have to use ______________________________

____

g) What do you have to do to get a job?

You ______________________________

____

KOHL VERLAG Der Verlag mit dem Baum www.kohlverlag.de
English: quite easy / Band 5 All about jobs - Bestell-Nr. 10 939

17 Practical training (work experience)

Exercise 1: *Give informations about the practical training you have planned.*

a) When will the practical training be?

____

b) Where will you work? Fill in the name, address and telephone number of the company:

____

____

c) You will work as:

____

d) What kind of duties will you have?

- ______________________________
- ______________________________
- ______________________________
- ______________________________
- ______________________________

e) What tools you think you will work with?

____

____

f) What do you think you will especially like?

____

____

____

g) What kind of work you don‘t like at all?

____

____

____

17 Practical training (work experience)

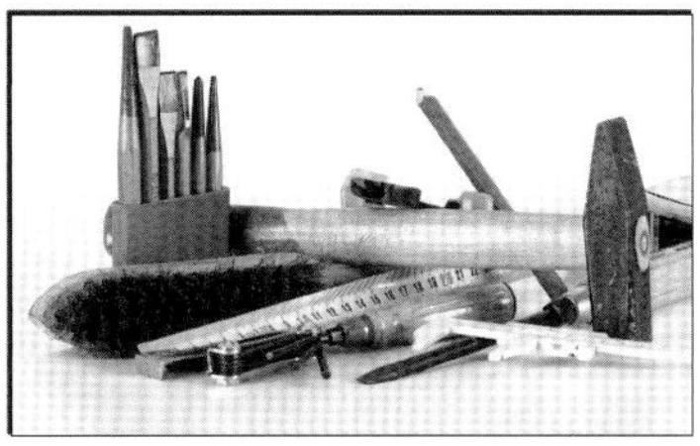

Exercise 2: *What can you tell us about your last practical training (work experience)?*

a) My practical training was from ____________________ until

____________________ .

b) The name of the company is ____________________

____________________ .

c) I worked as ____________________ .

d) My working day began at __________ and ended at __________ .

e) During the practical training I ...

- ____________________
- ____________________

f) I used the tools ... ____________________

____________________ .

g) It was easy to ... ____________________

____________________ .

h) It was difficult to ... ____________________

____________________ .

i) I liked to ....____________________ .

But I didn't like to ____________________ .

j) Now I am (not) sure ... ____________________

____________________ .

English: quite easy / Band 5
All about jobs - Bestell-Nr. 10 939
KOHL VERLAG Der Verlag mit dem Baum
www.kohlverlag.de

18 An interview in a company

Exercise 1: *Read the following dialogue between a reporter and Alexander Koch.*

Robert Walter	**Alexander Koch**
1. “Good morning! My name is Robert Walter.“	**2.** “Hello!“
3. “May I ask you some questions?“	**4.** “Yes,sure.“
5. “What‘s your name?“	**6.** “My name is Alexander Koch.
7. “What‘s your job?	**8.** “I am a trainee, I want to become a baker.“
9. “Is it an easy job?	**10.** “No, it‘s not. You have to learn and work hard. But I like the job.“
11. “How many hours do you have to work a day?“	**12.** “I have to work 8 hours each day.“
13. “When does your working day start?“	**14.** “It starts at 3 o‘clock in the morning.“
15. “Oh, that‘s early!“	**16.** “But the end of my working day is already at 12 o‘clock (a.m.).“
17. “What are you doing at the moment?“	**18.** “I am cleaning the oven.“
19. “Did you do a practical training in this company?“	**20.** “Yes, I did.“
21. “My last question: How much money do you earn as a trainee?“	**22.** “I earn about 550 Euro a month.“
23. “Thank you for the interview!“	**24.** “You are welcome!“
25. “I wish you all the best for your future.“	**26.** “Thank you, bye-bye!“

KOHL VERLAG Der Verlag mit dem Baum
English: quite easy / Band 5
All about jobs - Bestell-Nr. 10 939
www.kohlverlag.de

18 An interview in a company

Exercise 2: *Translate the interview into German.*

1. ______________________________
____

2. ______________________________
____

3. ______________________________
____

4. ______________________________
____

5. ______________________________
____

6. ______________________________
____

7. ______________________________
____

8. ______________________________
____

9. ______________________________
____

10. ______________________________
____

11. ______________________________
____

12. ______________________________
____

13. ______________________________
____

14. ______________________________
____

15. ______________________________
____

16. ______________________________
____

17. ______________________________
____

18. ______________________________
____

19. ______________________________
____

20. ______________________________
____

21. ______________________________
____

22. ______________________________
____

23. ______________________________

24. ______________________________

25. ______________________________

26. ______________________________

KOHL VERLAG Der Verlag mit dem Baum
www.kohlverlag.de
English: quite easy / Band 5
All about jobs - Bestell-Nr. 10 939

19 At work (work experience, training, job ...)

Exercise 1: *What may be good at work, what may be bad? Write down different things.*

Good things:	Bad things:
Example: It's an interesting job.	Example: It's a boring job.

KOHL VERLAG Der Verlag mit dem Baum
English: quite easy / Band 5
All about jobs - Bestell-Nr. 10 939
www.kohlverlag.de

20 Getting a job

Exercise 1: *Read the following text and translate into German.*

Getting a job

Many people are out of work. Today it's not easy to get a job. You have to make big efforts to find a job.

First make up your mind: What kind of job are you interested in? Then you have to pick up any information you can find about it.

Find out: Are you indeed the right person for the job? Do you best to get a practical training in one or two companies. Among other things you have to be punctual, reliable and busy. If your efforts are big enough, you have got a chance to be employed.

Look for vacancies. Apply for a job at so many companies as possible. Make sure that there are no mistakes in your letter of application. Always try to talk to the personnel manager of the company.

At least: Don't get discouraged, when you get a refusal. Keep on trying.

Getting a job

Exercise 2: *Answer the following questions in complete sentences.*

a) Does everybody have a job?

b) Is it easy to get a job?

c) You need a job. What do you have to do?

d) What should you think about?

e) What charasteristics are important during a practical training?

f) How can you get a job?

g) Oh dear – a refusal. And now?

KOHL VERLAG Der Verlag mit dem Baum www.kohlverlag.de
English: quite easy / Band 5
All about jobs - Bestell-Nr. 10 939

21 Finding a job

You can apply by letter, personally and practically.
By letter means: You write an application.
Personally means: You have an interview in a company.
Practically means: You go for a practical training.

A good way to find a job is to gain working experience. During a practical training you can find out your skills and abilities. It's better to go to a company yourself and apply personally than sending them your application documents (letter of application, curriculum vitae, photograph, photocopies of certificates).

Prepare yourself well for the interview. If you apply personally, you have to take the application documents with you.

Who could know something about vacancies?
Try to
- talk to your parents and other relatives.
- ask friends.
- talk to your teachers.
- visit a job centre.
- read the advertisements in the newspaper and in the internet.

Other ways to find a job:

Exercise 1: *Translate the text into German. Write into your exercise book.*

Exercise 2: *Answer the following questions.*

a) *How can you apply for a job?*
b) *What's a good way to find a job?*
c) *What do you have to take with you if you apply personally?*
d) *Who could know something about vacancies?*

22 Application

Exercise 1: *Complete the following application.*

From: ______________________________

____

____

To: ______________________________

____

____

Date: ______________________________

Dear ______________________________,

Last week I read your job offer for a training post. You look for a __________ ______________________________. I am very interested in the job and herewith I apply for it.

At the moment I go to school ______________________________, but I will leave school in ______________________________.

During my work experience I worked as a ______________________________ ______________________________.

My class teacher thinks that I am fit for work. I am always punctual, reliable and hard-working.

You can get more information in my enclosed curriculum vitae.

I hope you will grant me a personal interview. Thank you very much in advance for your consideration.

With kind regards

____

KOHL VERLAG Der Verlag mit dem Baum
English: quite easy / Band 5
All about jobs - Bestell-Nr. 10 939
www.kohlverlag.de

23 Curriculum vitae

<u>Exercise 1</u>: *Complete the following curriculum vitae.*

1. Family name: ______________________________

2. First name: ______________________________

3. Date of birth: ________________ **4.** Place of birth: ________________

5. Nationality: ______________________________

6. Address: ____

7. Telephone number: ______________________________

8. Languages: ____

9. School education: ____

____

____

____

10. Favourite subjects at school: ______________________________________

11. Hobbies: ____

____

12. Skills: ____

____

13. Practical training(s): ____

____

14. Practised jobs: ____

____

15. Job targets: ____

______________________ ______________________

(Date) *(Signature)*

KOHL VERLAG Der Verlag mit dem Baum
www.kohlverlag.de
English: quite easy / Band 5
All about jobs - Bestell-Nr. 10 939

24 A job interview

Exercise 1: *You are Linda Hopkins and you have an interview with the personnel manager, Mr. Brown, of a big company. You apply for a job. Complete the interview.*

1. "Good morning."

2. ______________________________

3. "Come in and sit down, please. What do you like to drink? Tea, coffee or mineral water?"

4. ______________________________

____

____

____

____

5. "Now let's talk about your application. Please tell me something about yourself."

6. ______________________________

____

____

____

7. "Did or do you like school?"

8. ______________________________

____

____

____

9. "Why do you apply for a job in this company? Are you fit for the job?"

10. ______________________________

____

____

11. "What do you know about this company?"

12. ______________________________

____

13. "What are your special skills?"

14. ______________________________

____

____

____

____

24 A job interview

15. "Do you have any weaknesses?

16. ____________________

____

____

____

17. "Did you go for a practical training?"

18. ____________________

____

____

____

____

____

19. "When could you start working?"

20. ____________________

____

____

21. "Do you have any questions?"

22. ____________________

____

____

____

____

____

23. "Thank you very much for coming! Next week we tell you whether you get the job. Please have still patience."

24. ____________________

____

____

____

25. "I hope you have a nice day. Goodbye!"

26. ____________________

____

____

KOHL VERLAG Der Verlag mit dem Baum
www.kohlverlag.de
English: quite easy / Band 5
All about jobs - Bestell-Nr. 10 939

25 All about my favourite job

Exercise 1: *Complete the sentences.*

a) I want to become a ______________________________ .

b) In this job you have to ______________________________

______________________________ .

c) I have to ______________________________

______________________________ .

d) The tools I work with are ______________________________

____

______________________________ .

e) It's easy to ______________________________ .

f) It's difficult to ______________________________

______________________________ .

g) My working time is ______________________________ .

h) The training takes ______________________________ .

i) As a trainee you earn ______________________________

____

______________________________ .

j) I will apply for ______________________________

____

______________________________ .

26 The world of jobs

Exercise 1: *One of the 6 words doesn‘t fit in.*
Cross out the name. Why it‘s not suitable?

a) astronaut - football player - shop assistant - singer - artist - racing driver

____

b) cook - hairdresser - flower - gardener - cabinet maker - painter

____

c) cleaning woman - policeman - nurse - waitress - housewife - actress

____

d) hammer - knife - saw - screwdriver - baker - drill

____

e) bakery - liberty - grocery - laboratory - library - factory

____

f) to clean - to sell - to repair - to build - to write - to sleep

____

g) punctual - friendly - busy - lazy - powerful - cooperative

____

h) newspaper - letter of application - curriculum vitae - photograph - school reports - references

____

i) name - address - hobbies - skills - work experience - shoe size

____

j) keyboard - oven - processor - printer - screen - scanner

____

KOHL VERLAG Der Verlag mit dem Baum
www.kohlverlag.de
English: quite easy / Band 5
All about jobs - Bestell-Nr. 10 939

27 My life in ten years

Exercise 1: *Imagine how your life will be in ten years. Write down.*

1. Now I am ________________ years old.
2. I live in ________________________.
3. My home is ________________________________.
4. I am _____________________ married.
5. The colour of my hair is ________________________.
6. I wear ____.
7. I work as a ____.
8. In my leisure time ____
   ____.
9. I spend my holidays ____
   ____.
10. Above all I like ____
    ____.

Exercise 2: *Try to find own sentences.*

____

____

____

____

____

____

____

KOHL VERLAG Der Verlag mit dem Baum
www.kohlverlag.de
English: quite easy / Band 5
All about jobs - Bestell-Nr. 10 939

28 Vocabulary test

Vocabulary test number ____________ Name: ________________________

English date: __________________________________

	English:	German:
a)	work	
b)	to be out of work	
c)	to have a job	
d)	company	
e)	to earn money	
f)	tool	
g)	to go to work	
h)	to search for work	
i)	to do a practical training	
j)	trainee	
k)	training post	
l)	training period	
m)	to train to be a	
n)	application	
o)	to apply for	
p)	curriculum vitae	
q)	skill	
r)	target	
s)	job offer	
t)	fit for work	
u)	punctual	
v)	reliable	
w)	busy	
x)	interview	
y)	refusal	

English: quite easy / Band 5
All about jobs - Bestell-Nr. 10 939
KOHL VERLAG Der Verlag mit dem Baum
www.kohlverlag.de

29 “What can you tell us about ... ?“ – a game

Spielregeln

Die Spieler sollen in englischer Sprache erzählen, was sie zu den auf dem Spielplan genannten 16 Themen wissen.

Es gibt mehrere Möglichkeiten zu ermitteln, welches Thema jeweils behandelt wird:

- Die Themen werden in der auf dem Spielplan vorgegebenen Reihenfolge bearbeitet.
- Der Spieler, der an der Reihe ist, sucht sich ein bisher noch nicht besprochenes Thema aus.
- Mit Hilfe von zwei Zahlenwürfeln (entweder zwei vierflächige Zahlenwürfel mit den Augenzahlen 1 - 4 oder zwei sechsflächige Zahlenwürfel mit den Augenzahlen 1 - 6) wird bestimmt, zu welchem Thema etwas gesagt werden soll.
  Das eine Würfelergebnis legt die waagerechte Koordinate, das andere Würfelergebnis die senkrechte Koordinate des Feldes auf dem Spielplan fest.
  Wer gemäß Würfelergebnis auf keinem Feld bzw. auf einem unbeschrifteten Feld des Spielplans landet, hat Glück und bekommt einen oder mehrere Punkte.

Für jeden korrekten Satz zu einem genannten Thema erhält der jeweilige Spieler einen Punkt. **Vorschlag:** Wer dran ist, kann zu einem Thema jeweils maximal 3 oder 5 bzw. 10 Punkte erringen (je nach Vereinbarung vor Spielbeginn).

Wer zum Schluss die meisten Punkte hat, ist der Sieger.

Weitere Themen können in das Spiel aufgenommen werden. Diese lassen sich auf den Blanko-Feldern des Spielplans notieren.

English: quite easy / Band 5
All about jobs - Bestell-Nr. 10 939
www.kohlverlag.de

29 "What can you tell us about ... ?" – a game

Spielplan

	1	2	3	4	
1	dream jobs	ordinary jobs	tools	computers	1
2	a working day	the world of jobs (adjectives)	opposites in the world of jobs	expectations in a job	2
3	a job	your last practical training	an interview	getting a job	3
4	application documents	the curriculum vitae	your favourite job	your life in ten years	4
5					5
6					6
	1	2	3	4	

KOHL VERLAG Der Verlag mit dem Baum
www.kohlverlag.de
English: quite easy / Band 5
All about jobs - Bestell-Nr. 10 939

30 Repetition

Name: ______________________ Date: ______________________

Exercise 1: *What can you tell (us) about dream jobs? Complete the centences.*

a) Dreams are ____.

b) You can dream of ____.

c) _________________________ and _______________________ are

_______________________.

d) Other dream jobs are ______________________________________.

e) Many girls dream to become _________________________________.

f) Others dream to be ____.

g) Some boys want to become __________________________________.

h) Others dream to be ____.

i) My dream job is ____.

j) But it's difficult to ____.

Exercise 2: *What can you tell (us) about ordinary jobs?*

a) There are _____________________________________.

b) For example ____

____.

c) Girls often like to become ___________________________________.

d) Other girls want to be ______________________________________.

e) Boys are often interested in _________________________________.

f) Other boys ____.

g) My mother's job is ____.

h) My father is ____.

i) I hope that I ____.

j) The favourite job ____.

KOHL VERLAG Der Verlag mit dem Baum
www.kohlverlag.de
English: quite easy / Band 5
All about jobs - Bestell-Nr. 10 939

Repetition

Name: ______________________ Date: ______________________

Exercise 3: *What do you know about tools?*

a) At work you need ____.

b) Tools are for instance ____________________________________.

c) Small tools are ____.

d) The ____________________ works with ____________________.

e) A _______________________ uses _________________________.

f) The ____________________ works with ____________________.

g) A _______________________ uses _________________________.

h) In a tool bag are ____.

i) I already used ____.

j) At home ____.

Exercise 4: *What do you know about computers?*

a) In the working world you ___________________________________.

b) You should be____.

c) Parts of the computer are__________________________________

____.

d) There are also: ____.

e) You can ____.

f) Besides you can____.

g) Furthermore you can______________________________________.

h) It is possible____.

i) I have ____.

j) Sometimes ____.

KOHL VERLAG Der Verlag mit dem Baum
www.kohlverlag.de
English: quite easy / Band 5
All about jobs - Bestell-Nr. 10 939

Repetition

Name: ______________________ Date: ______________________

Exercise 5: *Betty works as a sailes assistant. How is her working day?*

a) In the morning ____.

b) She ____.

c) Then she ____.

d) Her working day starts at ___________________________________.

e) First ____.

f) Then ____.

g) After that ____.

h) Later on ____.

i) At last ____.

j) Her working day ends ______________________________________.

Exercise 6: *What charasteristics are important at work?*

a) You should be ____.

b) Besides you have to be ____________________________________.

c) Furthermore ____.

d) Moreover ____.

e) You should be ____.

f) As a ____.

g) A ______________________ is _______________________.

h) Work ____.

i) Be ____.

j) I am ____.

30 Repetition

Name: ______________________ Date: ______________________

Exercise 7: *What is the opposite?*

a) The opposite of “having a job“ is ______________________________.

b) You can work inside or ______________________________________.

c) Day shift is the opposite of ___________________________________.

d) The opposite of a full-time job is ______________________________.

e) The opposite of a dream job is ________________________________.

f) The opposite of a male worker is ______________________________.

g) The opposite of an employer is _______________________________.

h) The opposite of a trainer is __________________________________.

i) The opposite of busy is _______________________________________.

j) The opposite of to hire is _____________________________________

.

Exercise 8: *What kind of different expectations people have in a job?*

a) People have ____.

b) They want ____.

c) Many people ____.

d) Others ____.

e) Some ____.

f) Or they ____.

g) Another expectation _______________________________________.

h) I want to ____.

i) Very important to me is ____________________________________.

j) Besides I wish ____.

English: quite easy / Band 5
All about jobs - Bestell-Nr. 10 939
KOHL VERLAG Der Verlag mit dem Baum
www.kohlverlag.de

Repetition

Name: ______________________ Date: ______________________

Exercise 9: *You are a baker. Tell your friends about this job.*

a) ______________________ is a ______________________.

b) As a baker you have to be ______________________.

c) At work you ______________________.

d) You have to ______________________.

e) And you ______________________.

f) Moreover you ______________________.

g) You use ______________________

______________________.

h) Good is ______________________.

i) Bad is ______________________.

j) I like/don't like ______________________.

Exercise 10: *Tell your teacher about your practical training.*

a) My practical training was from ______________________

to ______________________.

b) The name of the company ______________________.

c) I worked as ______________________.

d) The working day started ______________________.

e) My duties were to ______________________

______________________.

f) I used such tools ______________________.

g) It was easy to ______________________.

h) It was difficult to ______________________.

i) I liked ______________________.

j) Now I am (not) sure ______________________.

KOHL VERLAG Der Verlag mit dem Baum
English: quite easy / Band 5
All about jobs - Bestell-Nr. 10 939
www.kohlverlag.de

Repetition

Name: ____________________ Date: ____________________

Exercise 11: *You are a reporter and you ask Alexander Koch, a baker in a big company, about his job. Write down the interview.*

a) I: ____.

b) Alexander Koch: ____

____.

c) I: ____

____.

d) Alexander Koch: ____

____.

e) I: ____

____.

f) Alexander Koch: ____

____.

g) I: ____

____.

h) Alexander Koch: ____

____.

i) I: ____

____

____.

j) Alexander Koch: ____

____

____.

KOHL VERLAG
www.kohlverlag.de
English: quite easy / Band 5
All about jobs - Bestell-Nr. 10 939

Repetition

Name: ______________________ Date: ______________________

Exercise 12: *What can you tell (us) about getting a job?*

a) Many people ____.

b) It is not easy to ____.

c) First make up your mind: What kind of job ______________________

____.

d) Find out: Are you indeed _____________________________________.

e) Apply for a job at ____.

f) You can apply by ____.

g) By letter means: You _______________________________________.

h) Personally means: You ______________________________________.

i) Practically means: You ______________________________________.

j) It is better ____.

Exercise 13: *What different papers contain your application documents?*

a) The first page is ____

____.

b) Another important document is _______________________________.

c) Other documents are ____

____.

d) Your application documents should be without ___________________.

e) In the letter of application you can _________________________.

f) I am interested in ____.

g) Herewith I apply ____.

h) At the moment I go to ____.

i) I will leave school ____.

j) During my practical training I ________________________________.

KOHL VERLAG Der Verlag mit dem Baum www.kohlverlag.de
English: quite easy / Band 5 All about jobs - Bestell-Nr. 10 939

30 Repetition

Name: ______________________ Date: ______________________

Exercise 14: *What do you know about the curriculum vitae?*

a) The short form for curriculum vitae is ______________________.

b) At first you have to write down ______________________.

c) The next is ______________________.

d) The following ______________________.

e) Another part ______________________.

f) Important is ______________________.

g) You should mention ______________________.

h) Write down something about ______________________.

i) Besides you should note down ______________________.

j) Finally you must ______________________.

Exercise 15: *What's your favourite job?*

a) I want to become a ______________________.

b) In this job I have to ______________________.

c) I have to be ______________________.

d) At work I use such tools as ______________________

______________________.

e) It's easy to ______________________.

f) It's difficult to ______________________.

g) The working time is ______________________.

h) The training ______________________.

i) As a trainee you ______________________.

j) I hope (to) ______________________.

Repetition

Name: ______________________ Date: ______________________

Exercise 16: *Imagine how your life will be in ten years.*

a) Now I am ____.

b) I live in ____.

c) My home ____.

d) I am ____.

e) The colour of ____.

f) I wear ____.

g) I work as ____.

h) In my leisure time I ____

____.

i) I spend my holidays ____

____.

j) Above all I like ____

____.

English: quite easy / Band 5
All about jobs - Bestell-Nr. 10 939
KOHL VERLAG Der Verlag mit dem Baum
www.kohlverlag.de

31 Class test 1

Name: ______________________ Date: ______________________

The world of jobs

<u>Exercise 1</u>: *Dream jobs – write down ten of them.*

______________________ ______________________

______________________ ______________________

______________________ ______________________

______________________ ______________________

______________________ ______________________

<u>Exercise 2</u>: *Jobs – what is the name of the job?*

a) A person who makes bread = ______________________

b) A person who prepares food = ______________________

c) A person who cleans rooms = ______________________

d) A person who cares for plants in parks = ______________________

e) A person who cuts hair = ______________________

f) A person who repairs cars = ______________________

g) A person who builds the walls of houses = ______________________

h) A person who works with brushes and colours = ______________________

i) A person who makes clothes = ______________________

j) A person who sells goods in a shop = ______________________

KOHL VERLAG Der Verlag mit dem Baum www.kohlverlag.de
English: quite easy / Band 5
All about jobs - Bestell-Nr. 10 939

31 **Class test 1**

Name: ______________________ Date: ______________________

Exercise 3: *At work – what do working persons do?*

They ______________________ They ______________________

They ______________________ They ______________________

They ______________________ They ______________________

They ______________________ They ______________________

They ______________________ They ______________________

Exercise 4: *Tools – write down ten tools:*

______________________ ______________________

______________________ ______________________

______________________ ______________________

______________________ ______________________

______________________ ______________________

Exercise 5: **a)** *Adam is out of work. Imagine how he could spend his day.*

1. Adam gets up at ______________________________ .

2. Then he ______________________________ .

3. After that ______________________________ .

4. Later on ______________________________ .

5. At last ______________________________ .

English: quite easy / Band 5 - Bestell-Nr. 10 939
All about jobs
KOHL VERLAG Der Verlag mit dem Baum
www.kohlverlag.de

Name: ______________________ Date: ______________________

b) *Betty is a trainee. She works in a shop. Imagine how she could spend her workday.*

1. Betty wakes up ______________________________________.

2. Afterwards she ______________________________________.

3. Next ______________________________________.

4. In the evening ______________________________________.

5. Finally ______________________________________.

Exercise 6: *Turn the following ten sentences into Present simple.*

a) *I earned a little money in a shop.*
b) *The men worked in a hall.*
c) *The women cleaned the classrooms.*
d) *The trainer talked to a trainee.*
e) *Some boys and girls jobbed during the holidays.*
f) *George applied for a job.*
g) *Ann wrote an application.*
h) *Ron went to the job centre.*
i) *The pupils went for a practical training.*
j) *They got informations about the world of jobs.*

a) ______________________________________

b) ______________________________________

c) ______________________________________

d) ______________________________________

e) ______________________________________

f) ______________________________________

g) ______________________________________

h) ______________________________________

i) ______________________________________

j) ______________________________________

KOHL VERLAG Der Verlag mit dem Baum www.kohlverlag.de
English: quite easy / Band 5
All about jobs - Bestell-Nr. 10 939

31 Class test 1

Name: ______________________ Date: ______________________

Exercise 7: *Past simple ➔ Present progressive (Present continuous)*
Turn the following ten sentences into Present progressive.

a) *I earned a little money in a shop.*
b) *The men worked in a hall.*
c) *The women cleaned the classrooms.*
d) *The trainer talked to a trainee.*
e) *Some boys and girls jobbed during the holidays.*
f) *George applied for a job.*
g) *Ann wrote an application.*
h) *Ron went to the job centre.*
i) *They went for a practical training.*
j) *They got informations about the world of jobs.*

a) ____
b) ____
c) ____
d) ____
e) ____
f) ____
g) ____
h) ____
i) ____
j) ____

Exercise 8: *Adjectives – translate into English.*

a) pünktlich = ______________
b) freundlich = ______________
c) höflich = ______________
d) ehrlich = ______________
e) zuverlässig = ______________

f) sorgfältig = ______________
g) hilfsbereit = ______________
h) fleißig = ______________
i) verantwortungsbewusst = ______________
j) klug = ______________

English: quite easy / Band 5
All about jobs - Bestell-Nr. 10 939
KOHL VERLAG Der Verlag mit dem Baum
www.kohlverlag.de

Class test 1

Name: ______________________ Date: ______________________

Exercise 9: *Write down the opposites.*

a) The opposite of **to work outside** is ______________________________ .

b) The opposite of **an ordinary job** is ______________________________ .

c) The opposite of **employee** is ______________________________ .

d) The opposite of a **male worker** is ______________________________ .

e) The opposite of **part-time job** is ______________________________ .

f) The opposite of an **"ordinary job"** is ______________________________ .

g) The opposite of **unfit for work** is ______________________________ .

h) The opposite of **work-shy** is ______________________________ .

i) The opposite of **to dismiss** is ______________________________ .

j) The opposite of a **trainer** is ______________________________ .

Exercise 10: *Expectations – translate into German.*

a) The job must be interesting. = ______________________________

b) I want to have a regular employment. = ______________________________

c) I hope I don't have to work too hard. = ______________________________

d) I need a rest. = ______________________________

e) I want to earn a lot of money. = ______________________________

f) There is a chance to be promoted. = ______________________________

g) It is a respected job. = ______________________________

h) I have got a lot of fun at work. = ______________________________

i) I like to work together with nice people. = ______________________________

j) I have got various duties. = ______________________________

KOHL VERLAG Der Verlag mit dem Baum
www.kohlverlag.de
English: quite easy / Band 5
All about jobs - Bestell-Nr. 10 939

32 Class test 2

Name: ______________________ Date: ______________________

The world of jobs

Exercise 1: *What does he or she do?*

a) The doctor ____ .

b) The nurse ____ .

c) The teacher ____ .

d) The secretary ____ .

e) The policeman ____ .

f) The postman ____ .

g) The bank clerk ____ .

h) The waitress/waiter ____ .

i) The cabinet maker ____ .

j) The taxi driver ____ .

Exercise 2: *An interview in a company – write down 10 questions which you would ask a trainee, worker or manager?*

____

____

____

____

____

____

____

____

____

____

KOHL VERLAG Der Verlag mit dem Baum www.kohlverlag.de
English: quite easy / Band 5
All about jobs - Bestell-Nr. 10 939

Class test 2

Name: ______________________ Date: ______________________

Exercise 3: *You like your job/You don't like your job.*

a) *I like my job, because ...*

____

____

____

____

____

____

b) *I don't like my job, because ...*

____

____

____

____

____

____

Exercise 4: *Translate into German.*

a) favourite job = ________________

b) practical training = ________________

c) trainee = ________________

d) training post = ________________

e) period of training = ________________

f) application = ________________

g) curriculum vitae =

____

h) skill = ________________

i) job offer = ________________

j) interview =

____

English: quite easy / Band 5
All about jobs - Bestell-Nr. 10 939
KOHL VERLAG Der Verlag mit dem Baum
www.kohlverlag.de

Class test 2

Name: ______________________ Date: ______________________

Exercise 5: *What can you do to find a job?*

I can ____ .

I can ____ .

I can ____ .

I can ____ .

I can ____ .

I can ____ .

I can ____ .

I can ____ .

I can ____ .

I can ____ .

Exercise 6: *An application – complete the following sentences.*

a) I am interested in ______________________________________ .

b) Herewith I apply ______________________________________ .

c) At the moment I go to ______________________________________ .

d) I will leave school ______________________________________ .

e) During my work experiences I worked as ______________________

____ .

f) My class teacher thinks that______________________________ .

g) I am always ______________________________________ .

h) You can get more information in ______________________________ .

i) I hope you will invite me______________________________ .

j) Thank you very much, I hope to hear from you, ____________________

____ .

KOHL VERLAG
www.kohlverlag.de
English: quite easy / Band 5
All about jobs - Bestell-Nr. 10 939

Class test 2

Name: ______________________ Date: ______________________

Exercise 7: *What belongs to a curriculum vitae?*

Exercise 8: *My favourite job – complete the following sentences.*

a) I want to become a ______________________.

b) In this job I have to ______________________.

c) I have to be ______________________.

d) I work with such tools as ______________________.

e) It's easy to ______________________.

f) But it's difficult to ______________________.

g) My working shift is ______________________.

h) The training takes ______________________.

i) As a trainee you earn ______________________.

j) I will (apply for)______________________.

English: quite easy / Band 5
All about jobs - Bestell-Nr. 10 939
www.kohlverlag.de

Class test 2

Name: ______________________ Date: ______________________

Exercise 9: *Which of the following sentences are true, which are false? Mark with a cross.*

	true	false
a) Pilot is a dream job.	☐	☐
b) Basketball player is an ordinary job.	☐	☐
c) Nurse is a job for men.	☐	☐
d) A doll is a tool	☐	☐
e) A bakery is a place to work.	☐	☐
f) Working people repair things.	☐	☐
g) In the world of jobs you should be unpunctual.	☐	☐
h) The curriculum vitae belongs to the application documents.	☐	☐
i) You have to mention your shoe size in your curriculum vitae.	☐	☐
j) In the working world you need knowledge about computers.	☐	☐

Exercise 10: *My life in ten years. Complete the following sentences.*

a) Now ____.

b) I live ____.

c) My home is ____.

d) I am ____.

e) The colour ____.

f) I wear ____.

g) I work as ____.

h) In my leisure time _____________________________________.

i) In my holidays _______________________________________.

j) Above all I like _______________________________________.

KOHL VERLAG Der Verlag mit dem Baum www.kohlverlag.de
English: quite easy / Band 5
All about jobs - Bestell-Nr. 10 939

33 The answers

2

1. **a)** Bäcker, **b)** Bankangestellter, **c)** Maurer, **d)** Metzger, **e)** Automechaniker, **f)** Zimmermann, **g)** Kassierer, **h)** Putzfrau, **i)** Koch, **j)** Zahnarzt, **k)** Arzt, **l)** Arzthelfer(in), **m)** Schneider, **n)** Gärtner, **o)** Friseur, **p)** Hausfrau, **q)** Tischler, **r)** Krankenschwester, **s)** Maler, **t)** Polizist, **u)** Brieftäger, **v)** Verkäufer, **w)** Taxifahrer, **x)** Lehrer, **y)** Kellner, Kellnerin
2. **a)** I want to be a cabinet maker. **b)** My father is a car mechanic. **c)** My mother is a housewife. **d)** They are still pupils.

3

1. **a)** doctor, **b)** dentist, **c)** doctor's assistant, **d)** nurse, **e)** teacher, **f)** policeman, **g)** bank clerk, **h)** cashier, **i)** shop assistant, **j)** architect, **k)** bricklayer, **l)** carpenter, **m)** joiner, **n)** painter, **o)** cleaner, **p)** baker, **q)** cook, **r)** waitress, waiter, **s)** hairdresser, **t)** dressmaker, **u)** postman, **v)** taxi driver, **w)** car mechanic, **x)** gardener, **y)** housewife
2. Individuelle Lösungen!

4

1. **1)** baker, **2)** florist, **3)** secretary, **4)** data typist, **5)** manager, **6)** machine fitter, **7)** typesetter, **8)** farmer, **9)** joiner, **10)** waiter, **11)** butcher, **12)** drawer, **13)** photographer, **14)** physiotherapist

5

1. **a or b:** architect, actor, baker, butcher, bank clerk; **c or d:** cook, car mechanic, dressmaker, doctor, dentist; **e or f:** engineer, electrician, farmer, fireman, florist; **g or h:** gardener, glazier, hairdresser, housewife, hatter; **i or j:** illustrator, interpreter, jeweller, judge; **k or l:** kindergarten teacher, keeper, lawyer, lorry driver, laboratory assistant; **m or n:** model, miner, minister, nurse, news agent; **o or p:** optician, postman, policeman/policewoman, painter, plumber; **r or s:** roofer, retailer, shop assistant, social worker, secretary; **t or u:** teacher, tailor, taxi driver, trader, undertaker; **v, w or z:** vet, waiter, writer, welder, zoo director

6

1. **a)** They clean rooms. **b)** They wash clothes. **c)** They cut hair. **d)** They bake bread. **e)** They prepare food. **f)** They serve drinks. **g)** They care for flowers. **h)** They feed animals. **i)** They build houses. **j)** They cut timber. **k)** They repair cars. **l)** They drive lorries. **m)** They controll the traffic. **n)** They deliver parcels. **o)** They transport heavy things. **p)** They sell articles. **q)** They sort products. **r)** They write letters. **s)** They photocopy papers. **t)** They talk to other people on the telephone. **u)** They count money. **v)** They medicate ill people. **w)** They take care of old people. **x)** They teach pupils. **y)** They make music.

7

1. **a)** Axt, Beil; **b)** Besen; **c)** Kamm; **d)** Brecheisen, Brechstange; **e)** Bohrer; **f)** Feile; **g)** Zollstock; **h)** Gabel; **i)** Hammer; **j)** Messer; **k)** Nadel; **l)** Pinsel; **m)** Kneifzange; **n)** Forke, Heugabel; **o)** Harke, Rechen; **p)** Säge; **q)** Schere; **r)** Schraubenzieher, Schraubendreher; **s)** Schaufel; **t)** Spaten; **u)** Schraubenschlüssel; **v)** Spachtel; **w)** Wasserwaage; **x)** Löffel; **y)** Maurerkelle
2. **a)** I already used: a bromm, a comb, a file, a fork, a hammer, a knife, a needle, a paint brush, a saw, a scissors
   b) In my tool bag there is a drill, a file, a folding rule, a hammer, a pincers, a saw, a screwdriver, a spanner, a spint level, a crowbar
   c) I also know a ballpoint pen (Kugelschreiber), a pencil (Bleistift), a punch (Locher), a paper knife (Brieföffner), a pocket calculator (Taschenrechner), a telephone (Telefon), a computer (Computer), a brush (Bürste), a cloth (Lappen), a chisel (Meißel) ...

8

1. **a)** A carpenter works with an axe. **b)** A hairdresser works with a comb. **c)** A car mechanic works with a drill. **d)** A cabinet maker works with a file. **e)** A housewife woks with a fork. **f)** A plumber works with a hammer. **g)** A cook works with a knife. **h)** A dressmaker works with a needle. **i)** A painter works with a paint-brush. **j)** A gardener works with a rake. **k)** A roofer works with a saw. **l)** A tailor works with a scissors. **m)** A electrician works with a screwdriver. **n)** A waitress works with a spoon. **o)** A bricklayer works with a trowel.
2. **a)** xxxxx

9

1. **1)** screen; **2)** keyboard; **3)** mouse; **4)** mouse pad; **5)** writing desk; **6)** swivel chair; **7)** joystick; **8)** modem; **9)** scanner; **10)** processor; **11)** web camera; **12)** printer; **13)** speaker; **14)** disks

10

1. **a)** You can read or write a text, listen to music, play games, watch pictures and films, chat with other people, send an e-mail to somebody ...
   b) I like to play games, to chat with other people and to send e-mails.
   c) A computer freak is somebody who is very interested about computers. He/She spends most of his/her time playing and working with his computer. He/She knows everything about computers.

11

1. **a)** Adam gets up at 11 o'clock. He has a shower and brushes his teeth. **b)** Then Adam drinks tea and eats ham and eggs. Afterwards he writes an application. **c)** After that he watches television. Adam gets bored. **d)** Later on Adam meets some friends in the city. They play football in a park and go to a pub. **e)** At last Adam comes back home and reads a magazine. He falls asleep at 1.30 a.m..
2. **a)** Betty wakes up early in the morning. She has breakfast at 6.45 o'clock a.m. **b)** Afterwards Betty goes to work by bus. On the way she buys the daily newspaper. **c)** She works as a shop assistant in an electric shop from 8.00 a.m. to 5.00 p.m.. She likes her job very much. **d)** In the evening Betty plays cards games with her parents. After that she rings her boyfriend. **e)** Finally the young woman goes to bed at 9.30 o'clock p.m.. She is very tired.

12

1. **a)** pünktlich; **b)** freundlich; **c)** höflich; **d)** ehrlich; **e)** zuverlässig; **f)** sorgfältig; **g)** sauber; **h)** hilfsbereit; **i)** aufmerksam; **j)** fleißig; **k)** verantwortungsbewusst; **l)** anpassungsfähig; **m)** entgegenkommend/kollegial; **n)** stark; **o)** widerstandsfähig; **p)** unermüdlich; **q)** gut organisiert; **r)** klug; **s)** selbstbewusst; **t)** unabhängig

33 The answers

12 2. I am punctual, friendly and polite. Furthermore I am honest and reliable. Besides I am very busy, ...

13 1. **a)** I am earning a little money in a shop. **b)** The men are working in a hall. **c)** The women are cleaning the classrooms. **d)** The trainer is talking to a trainee. **e)** Some boys and girls are jobbing during the holidays. **f)** George is applying for a job. **g)** Ann is writing an application. **h)** Ron is going to the job centre. **i)** The pupils are gaining first working experience. **j)** They are getting informations about the world of jobs.

2. **a)** I earned a little money in a shop. **b)** The men worked in a hall. **c)** The women cleaned the classrooms. **d)** The trainer talked to a trainee. **e)** Some boys and girls jobbed during the holidays. **f)** George applied for a job. **g)** Ann wrote an application. **h)** Ron went to the job centre. **i)** The pupils gained first working experience. **j)** They got informations about the world of jobs.

3. Individuelle Lösungen!

14 1. **a)** leisure time (Freizeit); **b)** to be out of work (arbeitslos sein); **c)** night shift (Nachtschicht); **d)** "ordinary" job (gewöhnlicher Beruf); **e)** employee (Arbeitnehmer, Arbeitnehmerin); **f)** male worker (Arbeiter); **g)** part-time job (Teilzeitbeschäftigung); **h)** unfit for work (arbeitsunfähig); **i)** unpunctual (unpünktlich); **j)** lazy (faul); **k)** dishonest (unehrlich); **l)** work-shy (arbeitsscheu); **m)** dismiss (entlassen); **n)** trainee (Auszubildender, Auszubildende); **o)** loss (Verlust); **p)** demand (Nachfrage); **q)** sale (Verkauf); **r)** cashless (bargeldlos)

2. **a)** Yes, I am. **b)** No, I am not (No, I'm not). **c)** No, I am not (No, I'm not) **d)** Yes, I am. **e)** No, I do not (No, I don't), **f)** I prefer to work outside. **g)** I want to become an employee.

15 1. **1. Pos.:** "I want to have a regular employment." **2. Pos.:** "It is a respected job." **3. Pos.:** "The job must be interesting." **4. Pos.:** "There are chances to be promoted." **5. Pos.:** "I want to earn a lot of money." **6. Pos.:** "I like to work together with nice people." **7. Pos.:** "I have got various duties." **8. Pos.:** "I have a lot of fun at work." **9. Pos.:** "I need a rest." **10. Pos.:** "I hope that I don't have to work too hard." **Other expectations:** "I can be creative at work." "I can work inside and outside."

16 1. **a)** I am interested in working as a joiner. **b)** You have to work 8 hours daily, that's about 40 hours a week. **c)** I could earn about ... Euros. **d)** The job training will take ... years. This period may be shortened by a half year. **e)** You make chairs, tables, doors, cubboards and other things out of wood. **f)** I have to use an axe, a file, a folding rule, a spirit level, a hammer, a pincers, a screwdriver, a saw, a drill ... . **g)** You have to be interested in this job. You should like wood and have mechanical skills. If your school report is not too bad and you already gained some working experience, you have a good chance to get a job as a joiner.

17 1. **a)** 31.3 - 25.4.2008; **b)** Karstadt Warenhaus GmbH, Osterstraße 119, 20259 Hamburg, telephone (040) 490 1-0; **c)** sales assistant; **d)** I will work 37,5 hours a week. I will have to transport and unpack packages and pockets. I will have to assort articles (for example clothes) and put them into shelves. I will have to put price labels on clothes and I will have to serve customers. **e)** I will use a knife, a scissors, a label pistol, a cash desk, a ballpoint (pen) ... . **f)** I think I especially will like to serve friendly customers. **g)** I don't like to tidy up and to stand around for a long time.

2. **a)** My practical training was from February 2007 until March 2007. **b)** The name of the company is Bengel & Engel, it's a nursery. **c)** I worked as a kindergarten teacher. **d)** My working day began at 9 o'cklock a.m. and ended at 7 o'clock p.m.. **e)** During the practical training I learned how to look after babies and little children. You should be not too strict, but you mustn't be too careless. **g)** It was easy to play games and to sing songs. **h)** It was difficult to mediate quarrels between children and to calm crying babies. **i)** I liked to play games with the children and to read stories to them. But I didn't like to feed the babies. **j)** Now I am not sure whether I shall become a kindergarten teacher ot not.

18 2. **1.** „Guten Morgen! Mein Name ist Robert Walter." **2.** „Hallo!" **3.** „Darf ich Ihnen einige Fragen stellen?" **4.** „Ja, sicher." **5.** „Wie ist Ihr Name?" **6.** „Mein Name ist Alexander Koch." **7.** „Was ist Ihr Beruf?" **8.** „Ich bin ein Auszubildender, ich möchte Bäcker werden." **9.** „Ist das ein leichter Beruf?" **10.** „Nein, ist es nicht. Du musst hart lernen und arbeiten. Aber ich mag den Beruf." **11.** „Wie viele Stunden müssen Sie täglich arbeiten?" **12.** „Ich muss jeden Tag 8 Stunden arbeiten." **13.** „Wann beginnt Ihr Arbeitstag?" **14.** „Er beginnt um 3 Uhr morgens." **15.** „O, das ist früh!" **16.** „Ja, das ist es. Aber mein Arbeitstag endet schon um 12 Uhr." **17.** „Was tun Sie jetzt gerade?" **18.** „Ich säubere gerade den Ofen." **19.** „Machten Sie in dieser Firma ein Betriebspraktikum?" **20.** „Ja." **21.** „Meine letzte Frage: Wie viel Geld verdienen Sie als Auszubildender?" **22.** „Ich verdiene ungefähr 550 Euro monatlich." **23.** „Danke für das Interview!" **24.** „Gern geschehen!" **25.** „Ich wünsche Ihnen alles Gute für Ihre Zukunft!" **26.** „Danke, auf Wiedersehen!"

19 1. **Good things:** having various duties; working together with nice people; learning a lot of new things; being creative; earning enough money; a short distance between my home and my working place; flexible working hours; getting praised for my efforts
Bad things: doing a monotonously work; working alone without getting any help; working without learning anything new; only following the orders of the boss; earning too little money; a long distance between home and my working place; fixed working hours; getting dismissed

The answers

20 1. Eine Arbeit bekommen. Viele Menschen sind arbeitslos. Heute ist es nicht leicht, eine Arbeit zu finden. Man muss sich sehr anstrengen, um einen Job zu bekommen. Zuerst musst du dir Gedanken machen: Welche Art von Arbeit interessiert dich? Dann musst du darüber so viele Informationen wie möglich sammeln. Finde heraus: Bist du wirklich die richtige Person für den Job? Gib dein Bestes, ein Praktikum in einer oder zwei Firmen zu bekommen. Unter anderem musst du pünktlich, verlässlich und fleißig sein. Wenn du dich sehr bemühst, hast du gute Chancen, eingestellt zu werden. Suche nach Stellenangeboten. Bewirb dich bei so vielen Firmen wie möglich. Versichere dich, dass im Bewerbungsschreiben keine Fehler sind. Versuche immer, mit dem Personalchef der Firma zu sprechen. Zuletzt: Lass dich nicht entmutigen, wenn du eine Absage bekommst. Probiere es weiter!

2. **a)** No, many people are out of work. **b)** No, it isn't. **c)** You have to make big efforts to find a job. **d)** First make up your mind: What kind of job are you interested in? Then you have to pick up any information you can find about it. **e)** You should be punctual, realiable, busy, ... If your efforts are good enough, perhaps you will be employed. **f)** Look for vacancies. Apply for a job at so many companies as possible. Make sure that there are no mistakes in your letter of application. Always talk to the personnel manager of the company. **g)** Don't be discouraged. Keep on trying.

21 1. Einen Job finden. Du kannst dich per Brief, persönlich oder praktisch bewerben. Per Brief heißt: Du schreibst einen Bewerbungsbrief. Persönlich heißt: Du hast ein Bewerbungsgespräch in einer Firma. Praktisch heißt: Du absolvierst ein Betriebspraktikum. Ein guter Weg, einen Job zu finden, ist Arbeitserfahrung zu sammeln. Während eines Betriebspraktikums kannst du deine Begabungen und Fähigkeiten herausfinden. Es ist besser, sich bei einer Firma persönlich vorzustellen als ihnen die Bewerbungsunterlagen zuzusenden. (Bewerbungsschreiben, Lebenslauf, Foto, Kopien der Zeugnisse). Bereite dich gut vor für das Bewerbungsgespräch! Wenn du dich persönlich bewirbst, musst du deine Bewerbungsunterlagen mitbringen. Wer könnte etwas wissen über freie Stellen? Versuche folgendes: - Sprich mit deinen Eltern und anderen Verwandten. - Frage Freunde. - Sprich mit deinen Lehrern. - Besuche eine Jobvermittlung. - Lies die Stellenanzeigen in der Zeitung/im Internet.

2. **a)** You can apply by letter, personally and practically.
b) A good way to find a job is to gain working experience. During a practical training you can find out your skills and abilities.
c) If you apply personally, you have to take the application documents with you.
d) Try to talk to your parents and other relatives, ask friends, talk to your teachers, visit a job centre, read the advertisements in the newspaper and in the internet.

24 1. **2.** "Good morning, Mr. Brown." **4.** "Thanks! I would like a water." **6.** "My name is Linda Hopkins. I live together with my parents and one brother. I still go to school, Kingstreet, but I will leave it in June 2009. My hobbies are music and dancing. Besides I like to meet my friends in my spare time." **8.** "Yes, I always liked school. At school you will be prepared for life. My favourite subjects are German and Mathematics, two very important subjects, I think." **10.** "I am very interested in working as a florist. I read that you are searching for a trainee. I think I am suitable for this job, because I am punctual, reliable, honest, friendly and busy. You can say: I love flowers." **12.** "Your flower shop is well-known. You have many customers. The employees are very friendly and make goodlooking flower-arrangements." **14.** "I'm good at using the computer and I gained some experience, especially with plants and flowers, in my mothers garden." **16.** "I am not so good in English and Sport." **18.** "Yes, I did. I worked as a florist and then as a gardener. During both practical trainings I could learn a lot about plants and flowers." **20.** "School ends in July. So I could start working at 1st August 2009." **22.** "When are the business hours of your company? **24.** "Thank you for the interview." **26.** "I also wish you a nice day."

25 1. **a)** I want to become a hairdresser. **b)** In this job I have to be friendly. **c)** I have to work carefully. **d)** The tools I work with are combs, scissors, hair clips, hair dryers ... . **e)** It's easy to wash somebody's hair. **f)** It's difficult to perm somebody's hair. **g)** My working time is about 8 hours each day. **h)** The training takes ... years. **i)** As a trainee you earn about ... Euros. **j)** I will apply for this job.

26 1. **a)** Shop assistant is no dream job. **b)** A flower is no job. **c)** A policeman is a man. **d)** The Baker is no tool. **e)** Liberty is no place where people work. **f)** To sleep is no activity at work. **g)** You should not be lazy at work. **h)** A newspaper is no application document. **i)** You should not write down your shoe size in your curriculum vitae. **j)** An oven is not a part of the computer.

27 1. **1.** Now I am 25 years old. **2.** I live in a village. **3.** My home is very comfortable. **4.** I am not married. **5.** The colour of my hair is blond. **6.** I wear modern clothes and I'm very well-dressed. **7.** I work as a bank clerk. **8.** In my leisure time I play tennis. **9.** I spend my holidays at the Mediterranean Sea. **10.** Above all I like to meet my friends.

28 1. **a)** Arbeit; **b)** arbeitslos; **c)** eine Arbeit haben; **d)** Firma; **e)** Geld verdienen; **f)** Werkzeug, Gerät; **g)** zur Arbeit gehen; **h)** Arbeit suchen; **i)** ein Betriebspraktikum machen; **j)** Auszubildende(r); **k)** Ausbildungsplatz; **l)** Ausbildungszeit; **m)** sich ausbilden lassen; **n)** Bewerbung; **o)** sich bewerben um; **p)** Lebenslauf; **q)** Fähigkeit, Fertigkeit; **r)** Ziel(setzung); **s)** Stellenangebot; **t)** arbeitsfähig; **u)** pünktlich; **v)** zuverlässig; **w)** fleißig; **x)** Vorstellungsgespräch; **y)** Absage

30 1. **a)** not forbidden; **b)** jobs; **c)** Football player and model are dream jobs. **d)** pilot or singer. **e)** a model; **f)** a singer; **g)** a basketball player; **h)** a racing driver; **i)** boxer; **j)** become a professional boxer

2. **a)** many "ordinary" jobs; **b)** baker, cabinet maker or policeman; **c)** a hairdresser; **d)** a waitress; **e)** a car mechanic; **f)** would like to be a cook; **g)** a housewife; **h)** a cleaner; **i)** will find a good job; **j)** is gardener

English: quite easy / Band 5
All about jobs - Bestell-Nr. 10 939
KOHL VERLAG Der Verlag mit dem Baum www.kohlverlag.de

The answers

30

3. **a)** tools; **b)** a hammer, an axe and a spanner; **c)** a needle, a spoon and a knife; **d)** The joiner works with files. **e)** A hairdresser uses combs; **f)** The gardener works with rakes; **g)** A car mechanic uses spanners. **h)** files, hammers and drills; **i)** a hammer, a broom and a scissors; **j)** we have a lot of tools
4. **a)** find computers almost everywhere; **b)** able to use a computer; **c)** the screen, the processor and the keyboard; **d)** the printer and the scanner; **e)** use the computer to read or write a text; **f)** listen to music; **g)** play computer games; **h)** to chat with other people; **i)** a new computer; **j)** I play computer games
5. **a)** Betty gets up at 6 o'clock a.m.. **b)** has breakfast; **c)** goes to work by bus; **d)** 8 o'clock a.m.; **e)** Betty talks to her trainer. **f)** she serves customers; **g)** She has lunch; **h)** she sorts articles; **i)** she tidies up; **j)** at 5 o'clock p.m.
6. **a)** punctual, friendly and polite; **b)** honest; **c)** you have to be reliable; **d)** you should be careful; **e)** busy, not lazy; **f)** you have to be clever; **g)** A doctor is responsible; **h)** hard; **i)** fair; **j)** powerful and cooperative
7. **a)** to be out of work; **b)** outside; **c)** night shift; **d)** a part-time job. **e)** an "ordinary job"; **f)** a female worker; **g)** an employee; **h)** a trainee; **i)** lazy; **j)** to dismiss
8. **a)** different expectations; **b)** to earn much money; **c)** want to have an interesting job; **d)** like to have a regular employment; **e)** like to work together with nice people; **f)** want to have much fun at work; **g)** is to have a respected job; **h)** get a regular employment; **i)** is that the job is interesting; **j)** to work together with nice people
9. **a)** Baker is a cool job; **b)** punctual and reliable; **c)** should be powerful; **d)** bake bread and cakes; **e)** make rolls; **f)** have to clean the oven; **g)** spoons and knives; **h)** that you can find a job easily; **i)** that you have to get up very early; **j)** the job
10. **a)** 15.1.2007 to 23.2.2007; **b)** is "Flowers And More"; **c)** a florist; **d)** at 7.30 a.m.; **e)** to tie bunches of flowers; **f)** as knives and scissors; **g)** pour water on plants; **h)** make flower arrangements; **i)** to work as a florist; **j)** (that) I want to become a florist.
11. **a)** „Good morning!"; **b)** „Hello!"; **c)** „My name is ... May I ask you some questions?"; **d)** „Yes, of course."; **e)** „What's your job?"; **f)** „I am a trainee, I want to become a baker." **g)** „Is it an easy fob?"; **h)** „No, it's not. You have to learn and work hard." **i)** „How many hours do you have to work a day?" **j)** „I have to work 8 hours each day."
12. **a)** are out of work; **b)** get a job; **c)** What kind of job are your interested in?; **d)** Are you indeed the right person for the job?; **e)** so many companies as possible; **f)** letter, personally and practically; **g)** write an application; **h)** have an interview in a company; **i)** go for a practical training; **j)** to go to a company yourself and apply personally than sending them your application documents.
13. **a)** the letter of application; **b)** the curriculum vitae; **c)** photocopies of certificates, school reports and a photo; **d)** mistakes; **e)** write down; **f)** the job, because ...; **g)** for it; **h)** ... School at ... Street; **i)** in June 2010; **j)** worked as a baker
14. **a)** vitae; **b)** your name; **c)** your date and place of birth; **d)** your nationality; **e)** your address and telephone number; **f)** your school education; **g)** your favourite subjects at school; **h)** your hobbies; **i)** your practical trainings; **j)** sign your curriculum vitae
15. **a)** bike mechanic; **b)** repair bicycles; **c)** punctual and careful; **d)** spanners and screwdrivers; **e)** clean a bike; **f)** centre a bike; **g)** 8 hours a day; **h)** takes ... years; **i)** earn about ... Euros; **j)** find a job as a bike mechanic
16. **a)** 26 years old; **b)** Hamburg; **c)** is very comfortable; **d)** married; **e)** my hair is black; **f)** modern clothes; **g)** a hair-dresser; **h)** go shopping or swimming; **i)** in Turkey; **j)** my daughter, my son and my husband

31

1. artist, basketball pro, model, pilot, singer, astronaut, computer expert, racing driver, scientist, news presenter
2. **a)** baker; **b)** cook; **c)** cleaner; **d)** gardener; **e)** hairdresser; **f)** car mechanic; **g)** bricklayer; **h)** painter, **i)** dressmaker; **j)** shop assistant
3. They drive cars. They serve drinks. They build houses. They take pictures. They cook meals. They write letters. They bring parcels. They sort articles. They arrest criminals. They teach pupils.
4. hammer, spanner, drill, comb, knife, screwdriver, saw, file, scissors, spoon
5. **a) 1.** 11 o'clock a.m.; **2.** drinks tea and eats ham and eggs; **3.** Adam watches television; **4.** he meets some friends in the city; **5.** Adam comes back home and reads a magazine

   b) 1. early in the morning; **2.** goes to work by bus; **3.** she works as a shop assistant in an electric shop from 8.00 a.m. to 5.00 p.m.. She likes her job very much. **4.** Betty plays card games with her parents. After that she rings her boy-friend. **5.** the young woman goes to bed at 9.30 p.m. She is very tired.
6. **a)** I earn a little money in a shop. **b)** The men work in a hall. **c)** The women clean the classrooms. **d)** The trainer talks to a trainee. **e)** Some boys and girls job during the holidays. **f)** Georg applies for a job. **g)** Ann writes a letter of application. **h)** Ron goes to the job centre. **i)** The pupils go for a practical training. **j)** They get informations about the world of jobs.
7. **a)** I am earning a little money in a shop. **b)** The men are working in a hall. **c)** The women are cleaning the classrooms. **d)** The trainer is talking to a trainee. **e)** Some boys and girls are jobbing during the holidays. **f)** George is applying for a job. **g)** Ann is writing an application. **h)** Ron is going to the job centre. **i)** The pupils are going for a practical training. **j)** They are getting informations about the world of jobs.
8. **a)** punctual; **b)** friendly; **c)** polite; **d)** honest; **e)** reliable; **f)** careful; **g)** helpful; **h)** busy; **i)** responsible; **j)** clever
9. **a)** to work inside; **b)** dream job; **c)** employer; **d)** female worker; **e)** full-time job; **f)** a dream job; **g)** fit for work; **h)** willing to work; **i)** hire; **j)** trainee
10. **a)** Der Beruf muss interessant sein. **b)** Ich möchte einen dauerhaften Arbeitsplatz bekommen. **c)** Ich hoffe, nicht zu hart arbeiten zu müssen. **d)** Ich brauche eine Pause. **e)** Ich möchte eine Menge Geld verdienen. **f)** Es besteht die Möglich-keit, befördert zu werden. **g)** Es ist ein angesehener Beruf. **h)** Ich habe viel Spaß bei der Arbeit. **i)** Ich möchte mit netten Leuten zusammenarbeiten. **j)** Ich habe abwechslungsreiche Aufgaben.

English: quite easy / Band 5
All about jobs - Bestell-Nr. 10 939
KOHL VERLAG Der Verlag mit dem Baum
www.kohlverlag.de

33 The answers

32

1. **a)** medicates ill people; **b)** cares for ill people; **c)** give lessons at school; **d)** writes letters at the office; **e)** controlls the public order; **f)** delivers letters and parcels; **g)** works in a bank; **h)** serves food and drinks; **i)** makes tables, chairs, doors, ... out of timber. **j)** drives people
2. May I ask you some questions? What's your name? What is your job? Tell me about your typical workday. What's difficult for you? What's easy for you? Do you like your job? When does your working day start and when does it end? How much money do you earn each month? Did you do a practical training in this company?
3. **Good things:** The job is interesting. At work I can be creative. I work together with nice people. I've got a regular employment. I earn quite a lot of money.
   Bad things: I've got difficult things to do. My job is boring. When I've got a problem, there is nobody to help me. My employer is not very friendly. I have to work on weekends, too.
4. **a)** bevorzugter Beruf, Lieblingsberuf; **b)** Betriebspraktikum; **c)** Lehrling/Auszubildende(r); **d)** Ausbildungsstelle; **e)** Ausbildungszeit; **f)** Bewerbung; **g)** Lebenslauf; **h)** Fähigkeit, Fertigkeit; **i)** Stellenangebot; **j)** Vorstellungsgespräch
5. I can go for a practical training. I can send my application to as many companies as possible. I can apply personally. I can talk to my parents and other relatives. I can ask friends. I can talk to my teachers. I can visit a job centre. I can read the advertisements in the newspaper. I can try to find a job in the internet. I can hand out leaflets.
6. **a)** your job offer; **b)** for the job; **c)** ... School; **d)** at June 2010; **e)** a cook and as a waitress; **f)** I am fit for work; **g)** punctual, reliable and hard-working; **h)** my enclosed curriculum vitae; **i)** for an interview; **j)** with kind regards ...
7. name, place of birth, address, school education, practical trainings, date of birth, nationality, telephone number, hobbies, work experience
8. **a)** cook; **b)** prepare food; **c)** attentive, flexible, cooperative, ...; **d)** spoon, knife, fork; **e)** fry eggs; **f)** make a fondue; **g)** varying from week to week; **h)** takes ... years; **i)** your earn about ... Euro; **j)** the job at several restaurants
9. **a)** true; **b)** false; **c)** false; **d)** false; **e)** true; **f)** true; **g)** false; **h)** true; **i)** false; **j)** true
10. **a)** I am an adult. **b)** together with my girlfriend in a suburb of Berlin; **c)** large and fine; **d)** very interested in music; **e)** of my car is red; **f)** light-coloured shirts and dark-coloured trousers; **g)** cook in a restaurant; **h)** I like to do al lot of sports (football, jogging, ...); **i)** I often go to the seaside; **j)** to play computer games

Fremdsprachenunterricht

English – quite easy!
Elementares Fördermaterial Englisch

Englisch ist die Weltsprache Nummer Eins. Weltweit wird in der englischen Sprache im privaten und öffentlichen Leben kommuniziert. Englisch ist in vielfältigen Lebenssituationen anzutreffen. Die Sprache gilt als leicht zu erlernende Sprache, zumindest wird dies behauptet. Die Schulwirklichkeit jedoch zeigt: So manche Schüler haben sehr große Schwierigkeiten mit dem Englischen. Vor diesem Hintergrund entstand diese neue Lernreihe "English – quite easy", in der in kleinen Schritten ("step by step") vorgegangen wird. Diese Übungsreihe ist vorgesehen für Anfänger im Erlernen der englischen Sprache, sie ist konzipiert für den elementaren Förderunterricht. Die Kopiervorlagen gingen hervor aus der Schulpraxis – und zwar aus der langjährigen Arbeit mit Haupt- und Förderschülern. Jetzt sind zwei weitere Bände erhältlich!

je 12,90 €

- **Let's start to speak English** — **Nr. 10 805**
  (46 Kopiervorlagen, mit Lösungen)
- **Let's go on speaking English** — **Nr. 10 806**
  (46 Kopiervorlagen, mit Lösungen)
- **Grammar for beginners** — **Nr. 10 848**
  (48 Kopiervorlagen, mit Lösungen)
- **From Germany to the UK** — **Nr. 10 849**
  (48 Kopiervorlagen, mit Lösungen)
- **All about jobs** — **Nr. 10 939**
  (48 Kopiervorlagen, mit Lösungen)
- **All about teenagers** — **Nr. 10 940**
  (48 Kopiervorlagen, mit Lösungen)

Die Vokabel-Trainer Englisch
Den englischen Grundwortschatz spielerisch erweitern

Beide Bände:
Nr. 40 089
nur **25,90 €**

In diesen Bänden werden die jeweils passenden Begriffe des Grundwortschatzes gelernt, gesichert, wiederholt und vertieft. Auf spielerische Weise wird dadurch der Wortschatz erweitert. Die zahlreichen Dominos, Memories, Puzzles und Übungsaufgaben sind schulartübergreifend optimal einsetzbar!

Band 1 *(1.-3. Lernjahr)* **Nr. 10 823** **15,80 €**
(62 Kopiervorlagen, mit Lösungen)

Band 2 *(4.-5. Lernjahr)* **Nr. 10 828** **13,80 €**
(44 Kopiervorlagen, mit Lösungen)

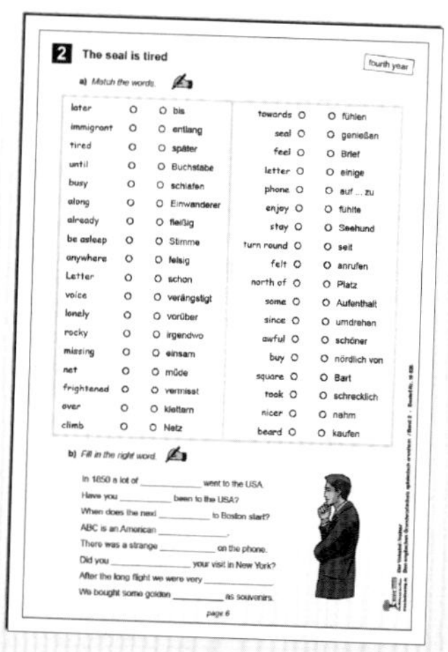

Belobigungsstempel

Eine positive Rückmeldung für gute Arbeit setzt zusätzliche Motivation frei! Machen Sie Ihren Schülerinnen und Schülern eine Freude!

„Very good"
Nr. 14 141 4,90 €

„Très bien"
Nr. 14 200 4,90 €

„Well done"
Nr. 14 206 5,90